Pablo Picasso

BY

PAUL ELUARD

TRANSLATED BY
JOSEPH T. SHIPLEY

PHILOSOPHICAL LIBRARY

NEW YORK

PRINTED IN THE UNITED STATES OF AMERICA

Pablo Picasso

*The author and the publishers wish
to thank Miss Dora Maar, Mrs. Louise
Leiris and Mr. Christian Zervos, who
have obtained most of the documents
published here.*

Dans ce haut lieu qu'est l'œuvre
de Picasso, j'ai voulu partager
les intarissables plaisirs qu'elle me
donne, j'ai voulu prouver, dans
les termes et dans les formes,
la confiance que l'homme fait
à l'homme.

In that high place which is the work of Picasso,
I have wished to share the inexhaustible delight it
gives to me; I have wished to testify, in the field of
terms and forms, to the faith man has in man.

TABLE OF CONTENTS

LIST OF ILLUSTRATIONS

Pablo Picasso

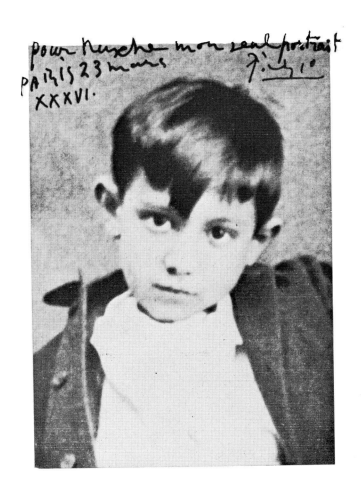

PICASSO AS A CHILD, 1887.

PICASSO, SELF-PORTRAIT, 1907.

PICASSO, SELF-PORTRAIT, 1902.

19

PICASSO IN 1901.

PICASSO IN 1935.

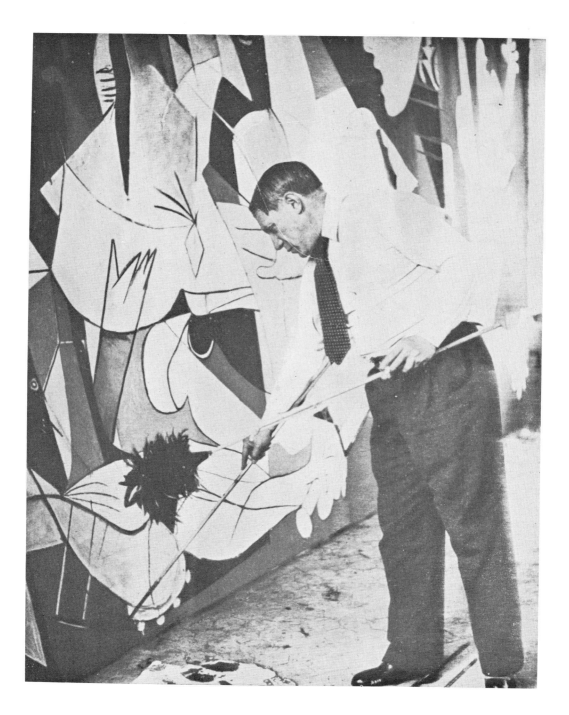

PICASSO IN 1937.

PICASSO IN 1940.

AT THE SEASHORE, 1938.

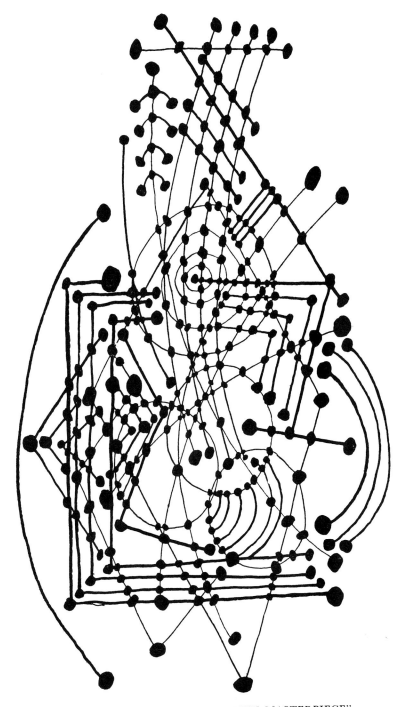

DESIGN FOR "THE UNKNOWN MASTERPIECE"

I SPEAK OF WHAT IS GOOD

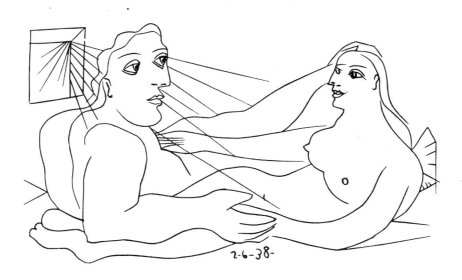

I SPEAK of what helps me to live, of what is good. I am not one of those that seek to wander off, to find forgetfulness, by loving nothing, by diminishing their needs, their tastes, their desires, by leading their lives—that is, life—to the hateful end of their death. I do not insist upon subjecting the world solely by the potential force of the intellect. I want everything to be sensible, real, useful, to me; for it's at this point I conceive my existence starts. Man cannot exist save in his own reality. He must be aware of it. If not, he exists for others but as a corpse, as a stone, or as manure.

29

Among the men that have most fully established their lives, of whom it cannot be said that they have passed along the earth without at once the thought that they will remain, Pablo Picasso stands with the very greatest. After having subjected the world, he had the courage to turn it against himself, sure that it would be not to conquer, but to find himself its size. "When I have no blue, I use red," he has remarked. Instead of a single straight line or a curve, he has broken a thousand lines that within him find their unity again, their truth. Scorning the accepted notions of objective reality, he has reestablished the contact between the object and the one that beholds it and that, consequently, thinks it; he has given us once more, in the most audacious, the most sublime, fashion, the inseparable proofs of the existence of man and of the world.

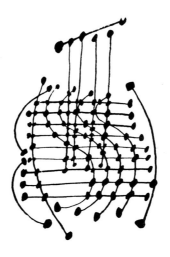

To those that cannot recognize to what extent Picasso's approach was revolutionary, we offer this explanation:

In general, thought tries first to distinguish between things and their relationships. Things provide concrete ideas; their relationships, abstract ideas; and for these, one must go from the subject to the object. Now, to traverse this road from subject to object requires a modicum of sympathy or of antipathy—whence spring ideas of value. This often leads animals, children, savages, madmen, and poets into errors or into the simplest illusions. They take a glass for a pit or a pitfall; a fire for a toy; the moon for a woman; a bottle for a club; a painting for a window. They err when they establish the relationship through antipathy; but when they rest it upon sympathy, it can be affirmed that that relationship serves as the basis of their truth. They are thus in turn strengthened by and victims of the faculty they possess, of comparing. Life is thus good and bad for them in turn, as it is for others. Some emerge from this stagnant state only to lapse into another state equally stagnant: animals are domesticated; children attain the age *of reason*; savages grow civilized; madmen are cured; poets forget. Some poets alone manage to rise beyond this sad alternative and, propagating their individuality, to transform the hearts of men by showing them, quite naked, a *poetic reason*.

PAINTERS have been victims of their medium. Most of them have been wretchedly limited to reproducing the world. When they have made a self-portrait, it has been by looking at themselves in a mirror, without thought that they themselves are a mirror. But they remove the silvering of it, just as they remove the silvering of the mirror that is the outside world, by deeming it outside. Copying an apple, they tremendously weaken its sensible reality. Of a good copy of an apple, it might be said: "You could eat it"—but nobody gets the notion to try. Wretched still-lifes, wretched landscapes, vain figurations of a world where nonetheless everything takes hold upon the senses of man, upon his mind, upon his heart. All that truly matters is to take part, to move about, to understand. Picasso, passing beyond all feelings of sympathy and antipathy, which are scarcely differentiate, which are not elements of movement, of progress, has systematically sought—and with success—to disentangle the thousand complications in the relationships of nature and man. He has attacked that reality which men declare intangible when it is only arbitrary; he has not conquered it, because it has taken possession of him as he has taken possession of it. A mutual, indissoluble presence.

The irrational, after having endlessly gone astray in dark or in blinding chambers, has, in the paintings of Picasso derisively dubbed cubistic, taken its first rational step. And this first step is at length a reason for its being.

ICASSO has created fetiches, but these fetiches have a life of their own. They are not merely intercessory signs, but signs in movement. This movement bears them to the concrete. Among all men, these geometric figures, these cabalistic signs—man, woman, statue, table, guitar—become men, women, statues, tables, guitars, more familiar than before, because comprehensible, appreciable by the mind as by the senses. What we call the magic of the design, of the colors, begins once more to nourish all that is around us, and ourselves.

IT HAS been said that to start with things and their relationships, for scientific study of the world, is not our right, it is our duty. It should have been added that this duty is the very duty of living, not in the manner of those that bear their death within them and are already walls or voids, but making one body with the universe, with the universe in movement, in process of becoming. Let thought deem itself not merely an examining or a reflecting function, but a motor function, a pandemic function, a universal function, the relationships between things being infinite.

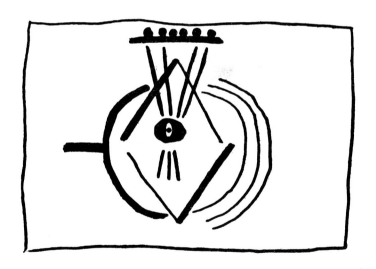

PICASSO desires the truth. Not that fictitious truth which would leave Galatea forever lifeless and inert, but a total truth that joins imagination to nature, that deems everything real and that, going endlessly from the particular to the universal and from the universal to the particular, accommodates itself to all the varieties of existence and of change, provided that they are new, that they are fertile.

IT'S ONLY when their complexities begin that objects cease to be indescribable. Picasso knows how to paint the simplest objects in such a way that before them everyone becomes capable once more, and not only capable but desirous, of describing them. For the artist, as for the wholly uncultured man, there are neither concrete forms nor abstract forms. There is only a communication between that which sees and that which is seen, an effort of comprehension, of relation—at times of determination, of creation. To see is to comprehend, to judge, transform, imagine, forget or forget oneself, to be or to disappear.

I am thinking of the famous picture of Picasso, *Woman in chemise* (page 48), which I have known for nigh on twenty years and which has always seemed to me at once most elementary and most extraordinary. The enormous and sculptural mass of that woman in her armchair, the head great as that of the Sphinx, the breasts nailed upon the bosom, are set in marvelous contrast—which neither the Egyptians, nor the Greeks, nor any other artist before Picasso could create—with the small-featured face, the wavy hair, the delightful armpit, the prominent ribs, the filmy chemise, the soft and comfortable armchair, the daily paper.

I am thinking of *My Pretty One* (page 45), which, for the first time, so brilliantly confirms the statement of Leonardo da Vinci: "The air is full of pyramids of radiating straight lines that start from every point of luminous bodies and that form angles more and more acute as they go farther and farther from their point of origin."

I am thinking of *Ma Jolie*, as stripped of colors as what one is accustomed to seeing, what one knows well. They do not surge out of space, they are space itself, contained by the limits of the picture, like spirals of smoke that fill an entire room, endless yet precise. Neither the limits of the picture nor those of the room restrain me; all the world is like this, composing itself, decomposing, and recomposing. O vague yet quintessential memory, I know what the night outside contains, what the invisible binds together, what forms it envelops. It is within me, easy-going or peremptory. I see within me. Out of its matrix Picasso has disengaged the gem.

ANDRÉ BRETON, in *Surrealism and Painting,* has written of Picasso: "It depends on a failure of will in this man whether the project we are engaged in be set back, or lost." Yes, for this man held in his hands the fragile key to the problem of reality. It was up to him to see that which sees, to liberate the vision, to attain clairvoyance. He has accomplished this.

LANGUAGE is a social fact. But may we not hope that one day design, like language, like writing, will become so; and with these will pass from the social to the universal? All men will communicate through the vision of things; and that vision of things will serve them to express the point that is common to them: to them, to things, to them as things, to things as them. On that day, a true clairvoyance will have integrated the universe to man—that is to say, man to the universe.

28.5.38

FISH AND BOTTLES, 1909.

HARLEQUIN, 1909.

MAIDEN WITH A MANDOLIN, 1910.

THE BOTTLE OF RUM, 1911.

44

MY PRETTY ONE, 1912.

THE TABLE, 1913.

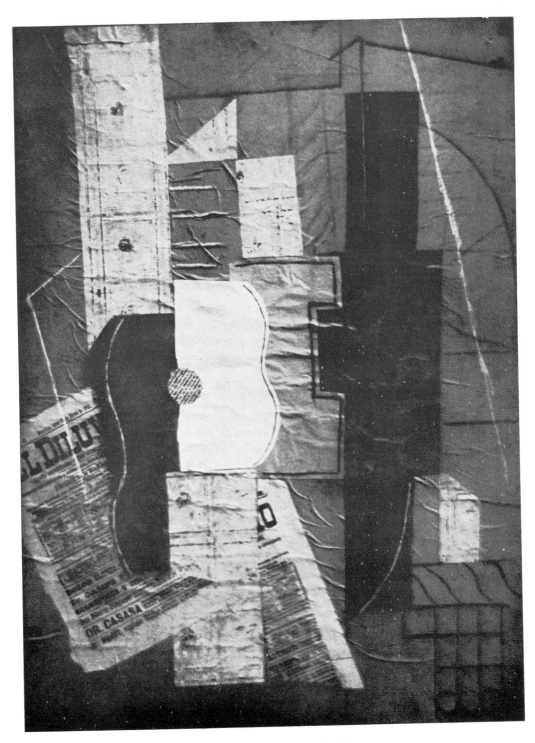

THE GUITAR (COLLAGE), 1914.

47

WOMAN IN CHEMISE, 1915.

THE PHYSICS OF POETRY

BEGINNING with Picasso, the walls crash down. The painter renounces his reality no more than the reality of the world. He is before a poem as the poet before a picture. He dreams, he imagines, he creates. And suddenly, behold, the potential object is born from the real object, and it in its turn grows real; behold, they form an image, from the real to the real, as one word with all the rest. One is no longer at a loss about the object, since all fits in, binds together, takes on value, takes its own place. Two objects separate only to find one another more fully in their remoteness, running the gamut of all things, of all beings.

51

The reader of a poem effectively illustrates this. He drinks at the source. This evening, his voice has another sound; the hair that he loves spreads in the air, or hangs heavy. It traces about the somber pit of yesterday, or buries itself in the pillow, like a thistle.

Then it is that the fine eyes start again, understand, and that the world lights up.

FIRST IN THE WORLD

To Pablo Picasso

Captive of the plains, madwoman in agony,
The light is lost on you; see the sky:
It has closed its eyes to withdraw from your dream,
It has closed your gown to snap your chains.

Before the knotted wheels
A fan bursts with laughter
In the treacherous blades of grass
The paths lose their reflection.

Can you not take the waves
Whose boats are almonds
In your warm caressing palm
Or in the ringlets of your hair?

Can you not take the stars?
Cross-lined, you look like them;
You dwell within their nest of fire
That multiplies your glory.

In the yawning dawn but one cry wants to burst,
A whirling sun streams underneath the bark.
It will fasten upon your closed eyelids.
O sweet, when you sleep, night mingles with the day.

PABLO PICASSO

The arms of sleep have hollowed in the night
The marvelous furrows that separate our heads.
Beside the diamond, all medals are false,
Under the blazing sky, the earth is invisible.

The countenance of the heart has lost its colors
And the sun seeks us and the snow is blind.
If we abandon it, the horizon has wings
And far off our regards will scatter errors.

END OF A MONSTER

You must see yourself die
To know that you still live
The sea is very deep and your heart quite shallow
Son of the earth eater of flowers cinder-fruit
In your breast the shades forever cover the sky.

Sun loose the cord the walls no longer are dancing
Sun leave to the birds impenetrable ways.

DESIGNS, 1937.

57

POEM BY PICASSO (ENGRAVING), 1936.

POEM BY PAUL ÉLUARD ILLUSTRATED BY PICASSO (ENGRAVING), 1936.

ETCHING FOR "THE SIEGE OF JERUSALEM," BY MAX JACOB, 1914.

To PABLO PICASSO

I

Good morning I have seen again who I do not forget
Who I shall never forget
And fleeting women who with their eyes
Made me a hedge of honor
Wrapped themselves in their smiles

Good morning I've seen my friends carefree
The men were light of weight
One that went by
His shadow changed into a mouse
Fled in the stream

I've seen the sky most large
The fair regard of men stripped of their all
Distant shore where no one disembarks

Good morning morning that opened gloomily
Black under the green trees
But that suddenly dipped in dawn
Slipped by surprise into my heart.

II

Show me that man always so gentle
Who said the fingers lift the earth
The rainbow that tangles the serpent that coils
The mirror of flesh where an infant pearls
And these quiet hands that go their way
Obedient clouds reducing space
Burdened with desires and images
One after another hands of the same clock

Show me the sky laden with clouds
Repeating the world hidden away beneath my lids
Show me the sky in a single star
I can well see the earth and not be dazzled
The hidden stones the phantom greens
Those great glasses of water those great blocks of amber
           of the countryside
The fire-and-cinder-works
The solemn geography of human limitations

Show me as well the black corsage
Drawn hair fathomless eyes
Of those dark pure maids who are but transient here and
furthermore to my taste
Who are proud doors in the walls of this summer
Strange jars without liquid full of virtues
Uselessly made for simple relationships
Show me those secrets that unite their temples
To those absent palates that lift the earth.

SOUP, 1902.

65

WOMAN WITH CROW, 1904.

66

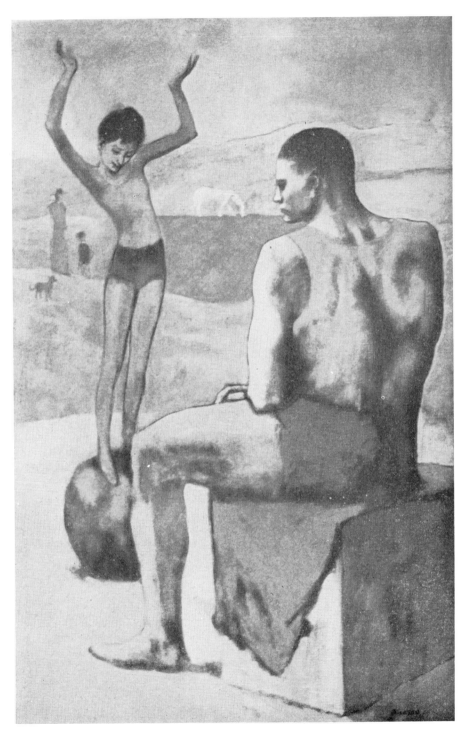

ACROBAT WITH BALL, 1904.

THE TWO SISTERS, 1904.

WOMAN IN CHEMISE, 1905.

69

SEATED WOMAN, 1905.

70

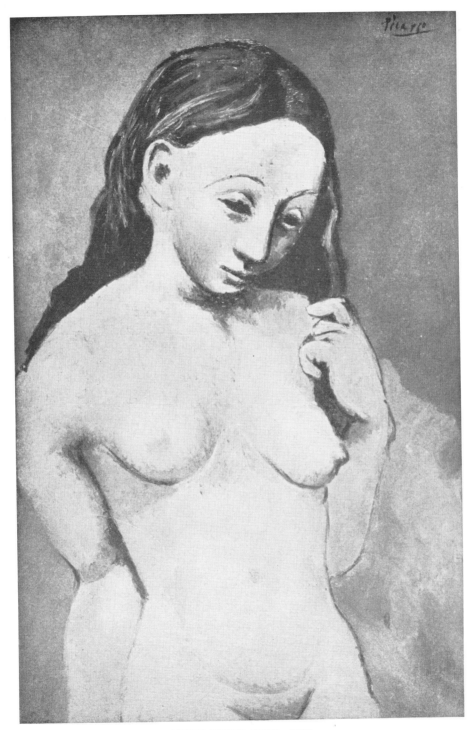

NUDE WITH HAIR, 1905.

NUDE WOMAN, 1907.

To PABLO PICASSO

I

Some have invented boredom others laughter
Certain ones fit life with a cloak of storm
They swat butterflies spit birds before the fire
And go off to die in the dark

You you have opened eyes that go their way
Amid natural things in every age
You have made harvest of natural things
And you sow for all times

They preached at you body and soul
You have put the head back on the body
You have pierced the tongue of the satiate man
You have burned the blessed bread of beauty
A single heart quickens the idol and its slaves
And amid your victims you continue to work
Innocently

There's an end of joys engrafted on sorrow.

II

A bowl of air buckler of light

Behind the three crossed swords of your regard
Your hair braids the rebel wind
Under your complexion upside-down the cupola and the
                    hatchet of your brow
Yield bare your proffered lips
Your nose is round and calm
The eyebrows are slight the ear transparent

At sight of you I know that nothing's lost.

III

An end of going astray anything can be
Since the table is straight as an oak
Color of monk's cloth color of hope
Since in our field small as a diamond
Is held the reflection of all the stars

Anything can be we are friends of man and beast
After the fashion of the rainbow

By turns fiery and frigid
Our will is of mother-of-pearl
It changes buds and blossoms not according to the hour but
          according
To the hand and the eye that we knew not ourselves
We shall touch everything we see

As well the sky as woman
We join our hands to our eyes
The holiday's new.

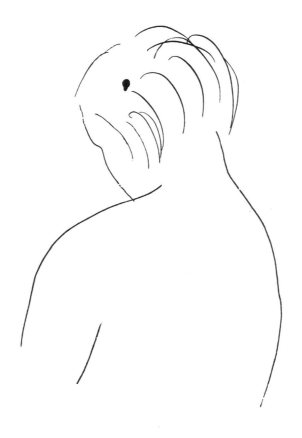

IV

The bull's ear at the window
Of the wild house where the wounded sun
An inner sun takes to earth

Tapestries of awakening the walls of the room
Have conquered sleep.

V

Is there a clay more sterile than all these torn newspapers
With which you set forth to conquer the dawn
The dawn of an humble object
You design lovingly that which awaits its being
You design in the void
As folk do not design
Generously you cut out the form of a chicken
Your hands played with your tobacco pouch
With a glass a bottle that gained

The infant world came out of a dream

Good wind for guitar and for bird
A single passion for the bed and barque
For fresh pastures and for wine that's new

The legs of the bathers bare the waves and strand
Morning your blue shutters close upon the night
In the furrows the quail smells of hazelnuts
Of olden Augusts and of Thursdays gone
Pied harvests full-voiced peasant women
Shells of the marshlands dryness of the nests

Countenance of bitter swallows in the raucous sunset

The morning kindles a green fruit
Gilds the grainfields cheeks hearts
You hold the flame between your fingers
And paint like a conflagration

At length the flame unites at length the flame brings salvation.

VI

I recognize the changing image of woman
Double star moving mirror
Negatress of the desert and of forgetfulness
Source with breasts of heather spark trust
Giving daylight to the day and her blood to blood

O hear you sing her song
Her thousand fancied forms
Her colors that make the bed of the countryside
Then go off to hue mirages of night

And when the caress takes flight
Immense violence remains

Insult remains with weary wings
Gloomy metamorphosis a lonely people
Whom ill-luck devours

Drama of seeing where there is nothing to see
Save oneself and what is like oneself

You cannot wipe yourself away
All is reborn beneath your even eyes

And on the basis of present memories
Without order nor disorder with simplicity
Rises the prestige of giving sight.

1938

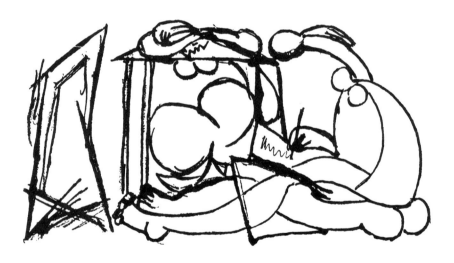

THE BULL'S EAR

The bull's ear at the window
And the light of today prism of force
On the victim's straw on the poor man's gold

On the table at the level of the wine in the bottle
The eye that seizes the mouth and kisses it
And watches it's delightful out

And watches in the gash of the bleeding workman
The bull the fine bull heavy with disasters

And watches it's delightful out
Beneath the sky of the mouth open to love
A heavy cloud that supports the sun
The workman's blood the wedding bread

The bull's flag
That the wind holds out like a sword.

THE GLASS OF ABSINTHE (BRONZE), 1914.

85

BOTTLE AND GUITAR (SHEET-METAL), 1913.

86

TABLE AND GUITAR FOR ST. RAPHAEL (WATER-COLOR), 1919.

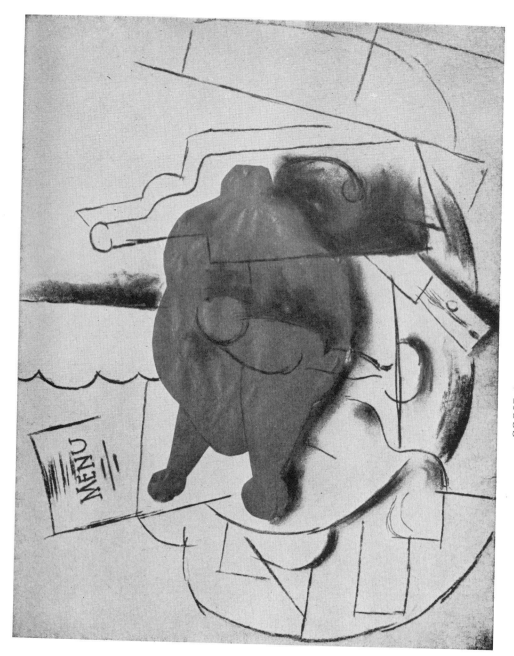

GOOSE (DESIGN AND COLLAGE), 1913.

88

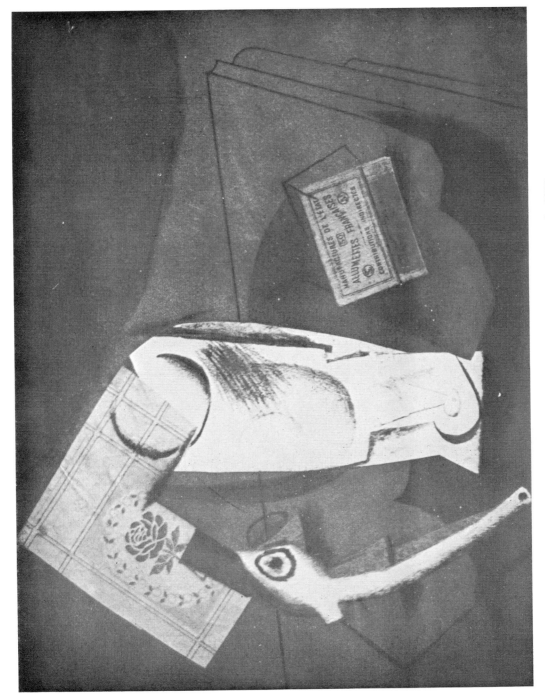

GLASS, PIPE, AND MATCHES (DESIGN AND COLLAGE), 1936.

89

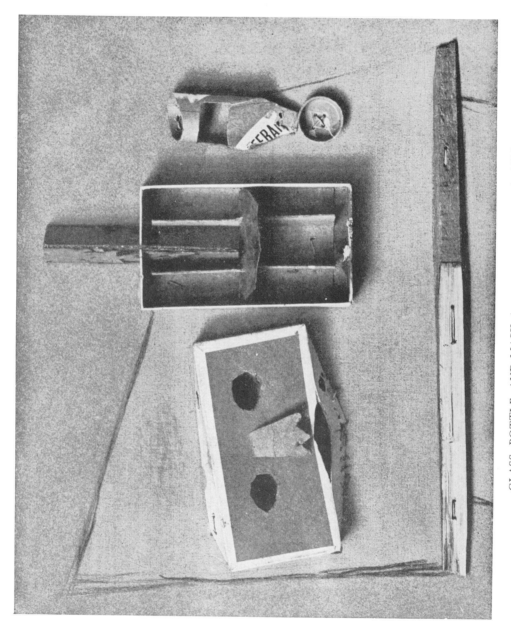

GLASS, BOTTLE, AND MASK (WOOD AND SHEET-METAL), 1936.

90

VASE OF FLOWERS, 1942.

91

COSTUME FOR "PARADE," 1917.

KNIFE CARVINGS, 1931.

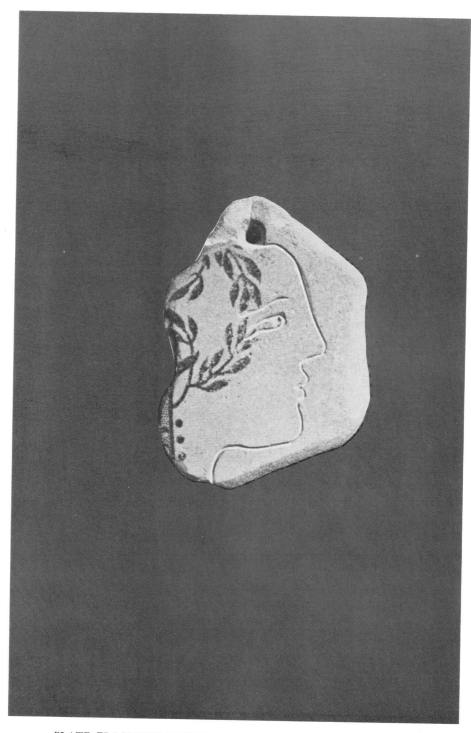

PLATE FRAGMENT FOUND IN THE SEA AND ENGRAVED, 1938.

94

TORN PAPER, 1943.

95

FEMALE BATHER, 1927.

PAINTED WORDS

To Pablo Picasso

To understand everything
Even
The tree that looks like a prow
The tree adored by lizards and by vines
Even the fire even the blind

To reunite wing and dew-drop
Heart and cloud day and night
Window and countryside everywhere

To abolish
The zero's grimace
That tomorrow will roll upon the gold

97

To cut off
The little ways
Of giants nourished on themselves

To see all eyes reflected
In all eyes

To see all eyes as beautiful
As what they see
Absorbent sea

To have folk laugh lightly
At having been hot at having been cold
At having been hungry at having been thirsty

To have speech
Be as generous
As embracing

To blend the bather and the stream
Crystal and dancer of the storm
Dawn and the season of breasts
Desires and childhood wisdom

To give woman
Thoughtful and alone
The form of the caresses
She has dreamed

To have the deserts be in the shadow
Instead of being in
My
Shadow

To give
My
Well-being
To give
My
Right.

THE RESCUE, 1932.

101

ENGRAVING, 1935.

102

GUERNICA, 1937.

103

THE WATCHING WOMAN (WASH DESIGN), 1942.

104

THE BATHERS, 1921.

105

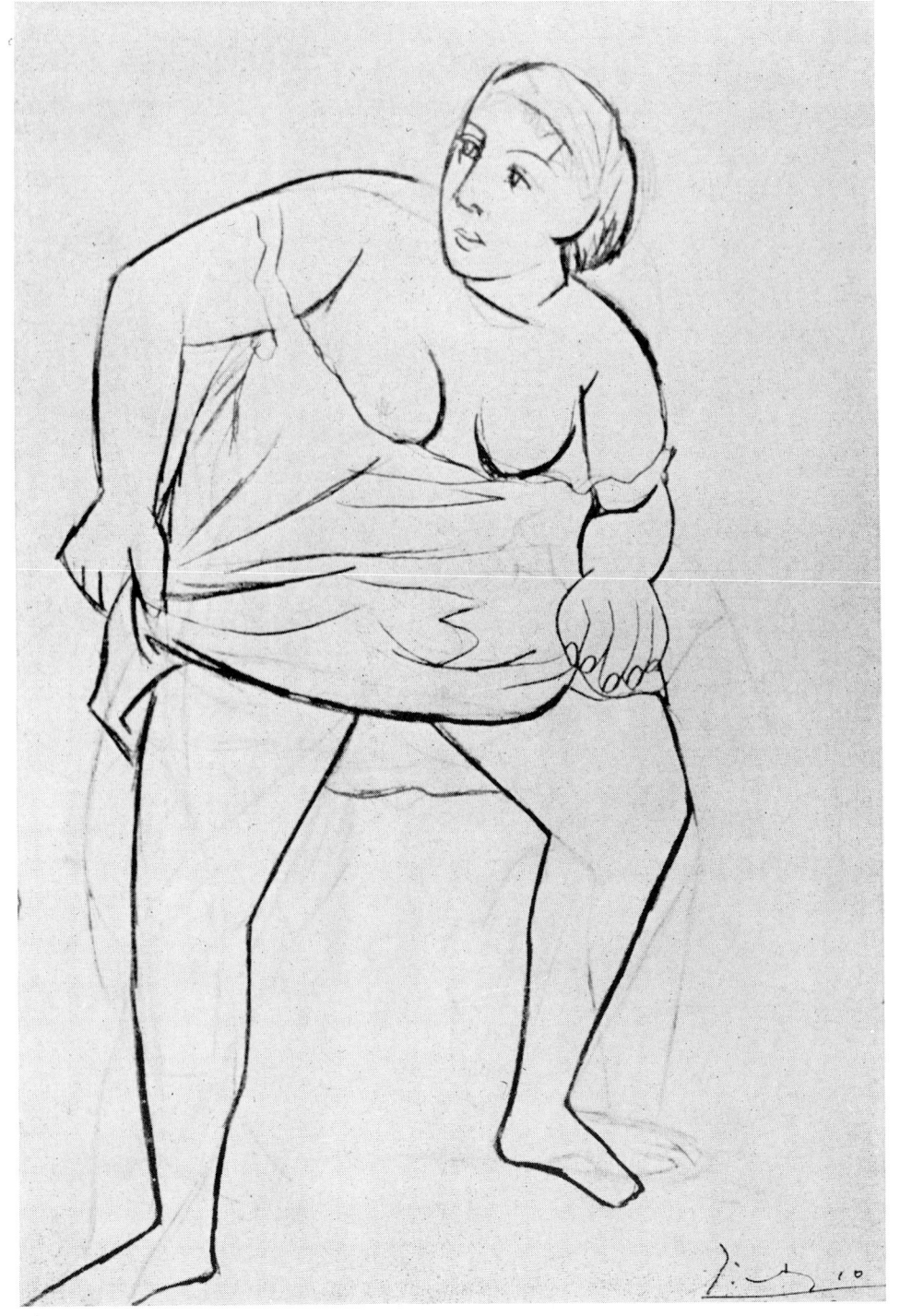

WOMAN IN CHEMISE, 1920.

INTERIOR (WATER-COLOR), 1934.

THE TWO LITTLE MAIDS, 1920.

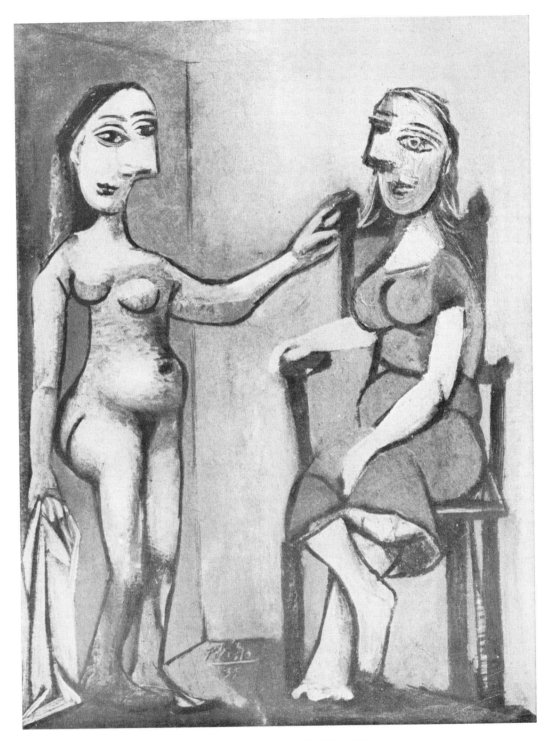

THE TWO LITTLE MAIDS, 1939.

WOMAN WITH COCK, 1938.

110

WOMAN IN THE GARDEN, 1938.

111

BIRD ON THE BRANCH, 1928.

IF YOU LOVE

If you love the intense cloud
Pour into every image
Its summer blood
Give laughter its golden lips
Tears its illimitable eyes
Great leaps its weight that slips away

For what you would come near
Light the dawn in the wellspring
Your binding hands
Can join the fire and ash
Ocean and mountain plain and foliage
Male and female snow and fever

113

And the wispiest cloud
The most banal remark
A thing that's lost
Force them to beat wings
Render them kin to your heart
Make them serve life entire.

FLIGHTS

I

Of the new day the great widespread birds
The virtue scarce more bright than yesterday
The virtue of pure air that my good luck embodies
The veriest good day all push the door
Sight is a perfect fatherland
Where I take in the tree the grass
The sun on the easy-resting earth
Faithful friend of the days of springtime and love
Of the days of summer autumn rest winter
Always the best of oneself.

II

Forest laden with summits and with space
Sea by turns wrinkled and relaxed
Man gifted with innumerable heads
I see you not
But by the short-cut of my darknesses
I am with you before I am with myself.

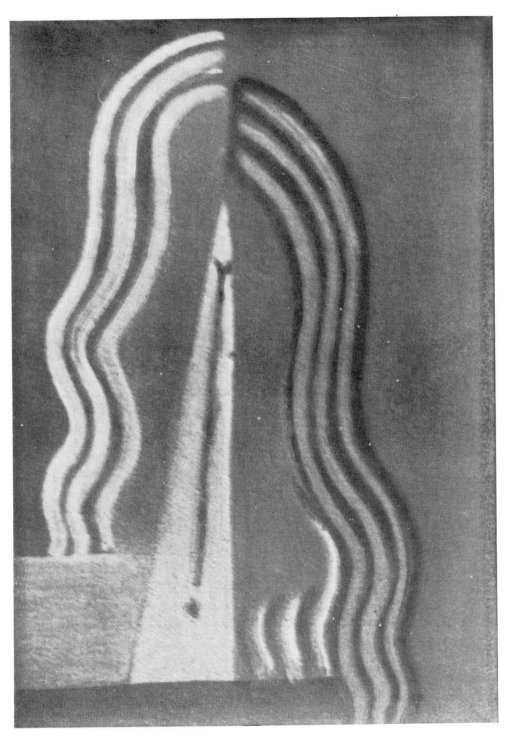

HEAD, 1914.

117

MOTHER AND CHILD, 1907.

118

HEAD OF A WOMAN, 1907.

119

STUDY FOR "NUDE WITH DRAPERY," 1907.

HEAD, 1909.

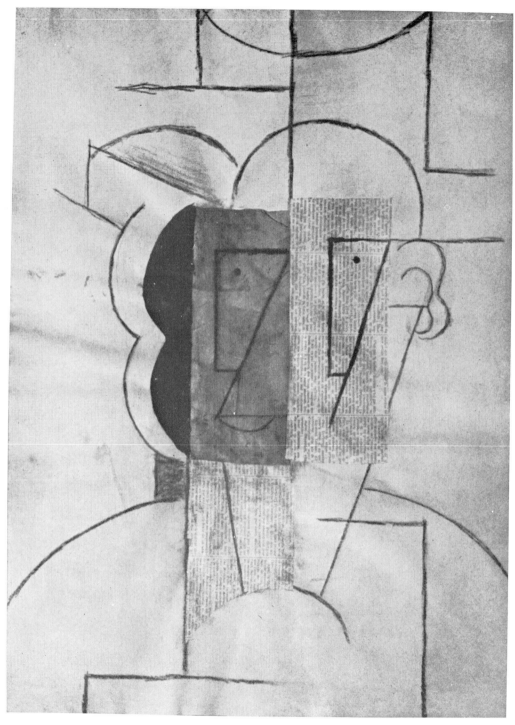

COLLAGE, 1913.

122

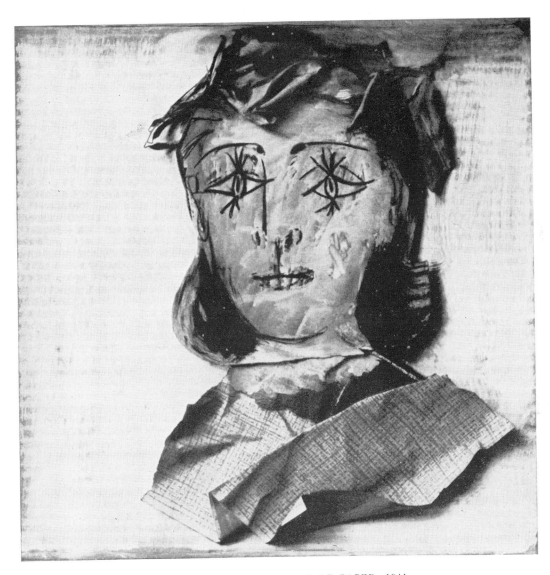

HEAD, PAINTED AND MADE OF PAPER, 1941.

123

HARLEQUIN HEAD, 1923.

124

STUDY FOR "GUERNICA," 1937.

ENGRAVED STONE, 1937.

126

MARINE, 1938.

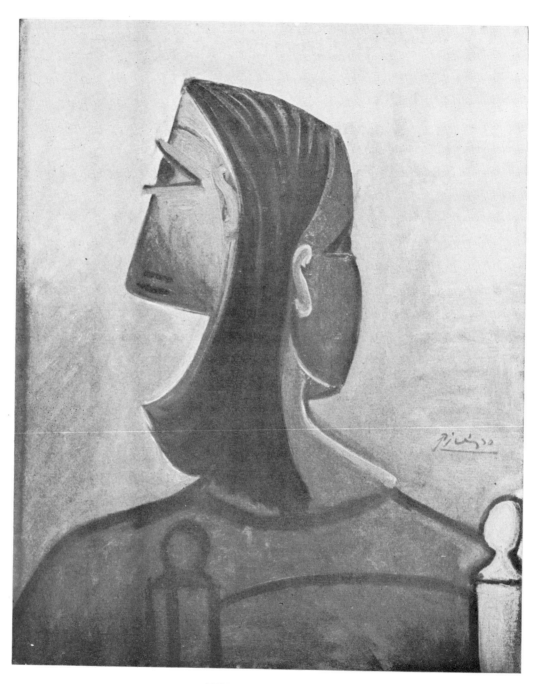

FEMALE BUST, 1939.

128

HEAD (WASH), 1941.

FEMALE BUST, 1943.

THE LOVERS (STUDY FOR "THE GAY BLADE"), 1943.

131

MARINE ROLLING A CIGARETTE, 1907.

132

OF OUR TIME

1

Upon my hand the muzzle of the bed
And I caress the bed

2

Line of the night horizon
Line still green and clear

3

This night to light my way
I see the eyes the heart of the survivors

4

In a city set and rude
As a broken paving stone

5

Overcome overcome slave
By an only too natural hate

6

But with open doors
Everyone laughs weeping

7

At the sight of a table
For those that are not hungry

But the sweetest of my homes
Tonight
Will be those of my friends.

OF OUR TIME

When our sky closes
Tonight
When our sky dissolves
Tonight
When the summits of our sky
Reunite
My house will have a roof
Tonight
It will be bright in my house
What a house is my house
A house a little everywhere
For all for any one at all.

PORTRAIT OF MAX JACOB, 1916.

137

PORTRAIT OF STÉPHANE MALLARMÉ, 1943.

138

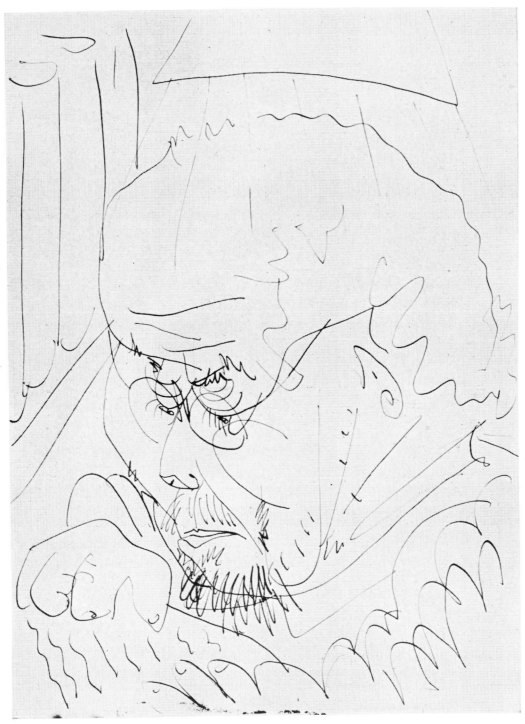

THE BIBLIOPHILE, 1941.

139

PORTRAIT OF AN OLD WOMAN, 1941.

THE ARTIST'S DAUGHTER (DESIGN), 1943.

141

WOMAN WITH CIGARETTE, 1901.

PORTRAIT OF JAIME SABARTES, 1901.

143

PORTRAIT OF MAX JACOB, 1907.

PORTRAIT OF GUILLAUME APOLLINAIRE (DESIGN), 1913.

PORTRAIT OF MADAME N. E., 1937.

MAN WITH LOLLYPOP, 1938.

147

PORTRAIT OF MADAME N. E., 1938.

148

PORTRAIT OF MADAME N. E., 1938.

PORTRAIT OF MADAME N. E. (DESIGN), 1941.

PORTRAIT OF MADEMOISELLE I. O., 1938.

151

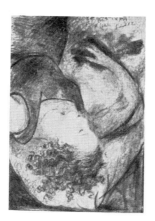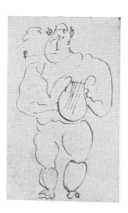

PORTRAIT OF MADEMOISELLE C. E., 1936.
PORTRAIT OF GUILLAUME APOLLINAIRE, 1915.
BOISGELOUP

152

TO PABLO PICASSO

A crowd of portraits
One is disdain the other is conquest
Another clear and lapping waters
Another bell of dew
The subtlest is a phantom
It goes along the ground and flatters its equals.

Here are the portraits of a sweetheart
Hiding the milk of her bosom
Under a blinding cloth
Before the watch-face of her countenance
A poor little sun trembles
Tender mirror

Mirror of all truth
Of every window in the morning
For an olden dance and blue
On the edge of two innocent eyes
Portraits sensitive and trusting
In good logic of love.

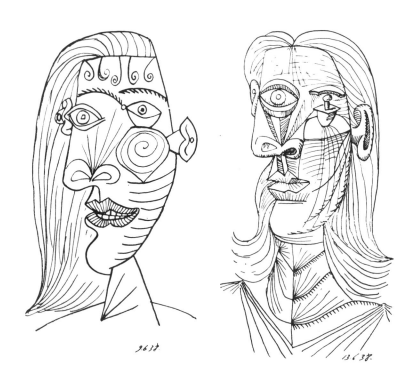

PORTRAIT OF MADEMOISELLE D.M. I (DESIGN), 1938.

155

PORTRAIT OF MADEMOISELLE D. M. II, 1942.

156

PORTRAIT OF MADEMOISELLE D. M. III, 1937.

PORTRAIT OF MADEMOISELLE D. M. IV, 1936.

158

PORTRAIT OF MADEMOISELLE D. M. V, 1938.

PORTRAIT OF MADEMOISELLE D. M. VI, 1936.

PORTRAIT OF MADEMOISELLE D. M. VII, 1939.

161

PORTRAIT OF MADEMOISELLE D. M. VIII, 1941.

ONE AND SEVERAL

In the mad restfulness of her sleep
It was snowing and the sky that made a tortoise
Gray as a blind lynx and treacherous as a hole
Judged the earth by its silence by its winter

In the mad restfulness of her sleep
There was the ocean with its hair dressed like a bee
There was the azure the brilliant clear the warmest
Of blood of fire of fine gold of kisses on the eyes

In the mad restfulness of her sleep
There were hands and eyes that fought
Fair hands adroit alive and trusting
And eyes to the past to the present to the future

Serving life and pleasure and hope.

SLEEPING WOMAN, 1941.

WASH DESIGN, 1936.

166

PORTRAIT OF MADEMOISELLE D. M. ASLEEP, 1937.

167

SLEEPING WOMAN, 1932.

168